Favorite Brand Name

4 INGREDIENT COOKBOOK

Publications International, Ltd.

Favorite Brand Name Recipes at www.fbnr.com

Microwave Cooking: Microwave ovens vary in wattage. Use the cooking times as guidelines and check for doneness before adding more time.

Preparation/Cooking Times: Preparation times are based on the approximate amount of time required to assemble the recipe before cooking, baking, chilling or serving. These times include preparation steps such as measuring, chopping and mixing. The fact that some preparations and cooking can be done simultaneously is taken into account. Preparation of optional ingredients and serving suggestions is not included.

Contents

Introduction

Welcome to simple, fast cooking without the fuss. With the 4 Ingredient Cookbook, you can now create tasty, exciting dishes without spending hours at the store gathering a long list of ingredients—or in the kitchen following complex recipe instructions. You can easily create most of these dishes, many of which are whole meals, in less time than it takes to go for carry-out food. And, preparing a home-cooked meal—especially one that is easy for the kids to help create—is a great way to get the family together and avoid the all-too-common tendency to order out.

The 4 *Ingredient Cookbook* is full of easy-to-follow recipes, many with four ingredients or less. Excluded from the count are those ingredients common to many recipes and found in most kitchens: water, nonstick cooking spray, salt and pepper. Also not counted are implements such as skewers and racks, and ingredients labeled as "optional" or "for garnish."

Cooking with these recipes can save you a great deal of time. Get the most out of this book by planning your meals in advance. Be sure to read through any recipes you're making before you go shopping, to be certain you buy all the needed ingredients.

Many recipes can be prepared so quickly that you can put together appetizers, side dishes or desserts while a main course is cooking. Some quick-assemble dishes take only a few minutes to prepare but require a longer time in the oven or slow cooker; others need time to marinate. Spend the extra time exercising, doing errands or relaxing with the family. That's what the 4 *Ingredient Cookbook* is designed to do: free you up to do other things!

Use the tips that are included in this book to streamline your preparation and cooking processes.

 "Quick Tips" tell you how to save time in the supermarket and the kitchen

 "Smart Tips" offer suggestions on cooking or ingredients that can help you to make a better meal

 "Serving Tips" give you ideas on how to simplify and enhance your meal presentation

Appetizers and Drinks

Start off a special meal by making a quick

and easy appetizer, or add an accompanying drink

to liven things up a little. It will heighten

expectations for the main dish. . . and everyone will

remember an event, not just a

meal. The little additions can

make big impressions.

*Shrimp and Snow Pea Appetizers with Currant
Mustard Sauce (recipe on page 12)*

Pace® Chili con Queso Bites

    4 eggs
    ½ cup PACE® Picante Sauce *or* Thick & Chunky Salsa
    ¼ cup all-purpose flour
    2 teaspoons chili powder
    1½ cups shredded Cheddar cheese (6 ounces)
    1 green onion, chopped (about 2 tablespoons)

1. Preheat oven to 400°F. Grease 24 (3-inch) muffin-pan cups. Set aside.

2. In medium bowl mix eggs, picante sauce, flour and chili powder. Stir in cheese and onion.

3. Spoon about **1 *tablespoon*** cheese mixture into each cup. Bake 10 minutes or until golden brown. Serve warm or at room temperature with sour cream and additional picante sauce if desired.

Makes 24 appetizers

Prep Time: *10 minutes*
Cook Time: *10 minutes*

V8® Bloody Mary Mocktail

    3 cups V8® 100% Vegetable Juice
    1 teaspoon prepared horseradish
    1 teaspoon Worcestershire sauce
    ½ teaspoon hot pepper sauce
    Lemon slices for garnish

Mix vegetable juice, horseradish, Worcestershire sauce and hot pepper sauce. Serve over ice. Garnish with lemon slices.

Makes 3 cups

Prep Time: *5 minutes*

V8® Bloody Mary Mocktail and Pace® Chili con Queso Bites

Shrimp and Snow Pea Appetizers with Currant Mustard Sauce

> 6 ounces fresh snow peas (about 36)
> 1½ pounds medium shrimp, peeled, deveined and cooked
> ¾ cup SMUCKER'S® Currant Jelly
> ¼ cup Dijon mustard

Blanch snow peas in boiling salted water for 45 seconds. Immediately drain and run under cold water.

Wrap 1 blanched pea pod around each shrimp and secure with toothpick.

Combine jelly and mustard; beat with a fork or wire whisk until smooth. (Jelly will dissolve in about 5 minutes.) Serve sauce with appetizers.

Makes 36 appetizers

Sugar 'n' Spice Nuts

> 4 cups assorted salted mixed nuts
> 2 tablespoons I CAN'T BELIEVE IT'S NOT BUTTER!® Spread, melted
> 3 tablespoons sugar
> 1 to 2 teaspoons ground red pepper
> 2 teaspoons dried coriander (optional)

Preheat oven to 300°F.

In large bowl, combine mixed nuts and I Can't Believe It's Not Butter! Spread; set aside.

In small bowl, blend remaining ingredients; stir into nut mixture. On ungreased baking sheet, evenly spread nut mixture.

Bake, stirring occasionally, 40 minutes or until nuts are golden.

Makes 4 cups nuts

Cheddar Tomato Bacon Toasts

Cheddar Tomato Bacon Toasts

1 jar (16 ounces) RAGÚ® Cheese Creations!® Double Cheddar Sauce
1 medium tomato, chopped
5 slices bacon, crisp-cooked and crumbled (about ⅓ cup)
2 loaves Italian bread (each about 16 inches long), each cut into 16 slices

1. Preheat oven to 350°F. In medium bowl, combine Ragú Cheese Creations! Sauce, tomato and bacon.

2. On baking sheet, arrange bread slices. Evenly top with sauce mixture.

3. Bake 10 minutes or until sauce mixture is bubbling. Serve immediately.   *Makes 16 servings*

Prep Time: 10 *minutes*
Cook Time: 10 *minutes*

Hot Buttered Cider

⅓ cup packed brown sugar
¼ cup butter or margarine, softened
¼ cup honey
¼ teaspoon ground cinnamon
¼ teaspoon ground nutmeg
    Apple cider or juice

1. Beat sugar, butter, honey, cinnamon and nutmeg until well blended and fluffy. Place mixture in tightly covered container. Refrigerate up to 2 weeks. Bring mixture to room temperature before using.

2. To serve, heat apple cider in large saucepan over medium heat until hot. Fill individual mugs with hot apple cider; stir in 1 tablespoon butter mixture per 1 cup apple cider.   *Makes 12 servings*

Prep and Cook Time: *15 minutes*

Crabmeat Spread

1 package (8 ounces) light cream cheese, softened
¼ cup cocktail sauce
1 package (8 ounces) imitation crabmeat

Spread cream cheese evenly on serving plate. Pour cocktail sauce over cream cheese; top with imitation crabmeat.

Serve with assorted crackers.   *Makes 1½ cups (12 servings)*

Hot Buttered Cider

Cheese Straws

½ cup (1 stick) butter, softened
⅛ teaspoon salt
   Dash ground red pepper
 1 pound sharp Cheddar cheese, shredded, at room
      temperature
 2 cups self-rising flour

Heat oven to 350°F. In mixer bowl, beat butter, salt and pepper until creamy. Add cheese; mix well. Gradually add flour, mixing until dough begins to form a ball. Form dough into ball with hands.

Fit cookie press with small star plate; fill with dough according to manufacturer's directions. Press dough onto cookie sheets in 3-inch-long strips. Bake 12 minutes or until lightly browned. Cool completely on wire rack. Store tightly covered.   *Makes about 10 dozen*

Fast Pesto Focaccia

 1 can (10 ounces) pizza crust dough
 2 tablespoons prepared pesto
 4 sun-dried tomatoes packed in oil, drained

1. Preheat oven to 425°F. Lightly grease 8×8×2-inch pan. Unroll pizza dough; fold in half and pat into pan.

2. Spread pesto evenly over dough. Chop tomatoes or snip with kitchen scissors; sprinkle over pesto. Press tomatoes into dough. Make indentations in dough every 2 inches using wooden spoon handle.

3. Bake 10 to 12 minutes or until golden brown. Cut into squares and serve warm or at room temperature.   *Makes 16 appetizers*

Prep and Cook Time: *20 minutes*

Cheese Straws

Tortellini Kabobs with Pesto Ranch Dip

Tortellini Kabobs with Pesto Ranch Dip

½ bag (16 ounces) frozen tortellini
1¼ cups ranch salad dressing
½ cup grated Parmesan cheese
3 cloves garlic, minced
2 teaspoons dried basil leaves

1. Cook tortellini according to package directions. Rinse and drain under cold water. Thread tortellini onto bamboo skewers, 2 tortellini per skewer.

2. Combine salad dressing, cheese, garlic and basil in small bowl. Serve tortellini kabobs with dip.   *Makes 6 to 8 servings*

Serving suggestion: For an even quicker dip, combine purchased spaghetti sauce or salsa with some finely chopped black olives.

Prep and Cook Time: *30 minutes*

Campbell's® Asparagus & Ham Potato Topper

4 hot baked potatoes, split
1 cup diced cooked ham
1 can (10¾ ounces) CAMPBELL'S® Condensed Cream of Asparagus Soup
Shredded Cheddar *or* Swiss cheese (optional)

1. Place hot baked potatoes on microwave-safe plate. Carefully fluff up potatoes with fork.

2. Top each potato with ham. Stir soup in can until smooth. Spoon soup over potatoes. Top with cheese, if desired. Microwave on HIGH 4 minutes or until hot.

Makes 4 servings

Prep/Cook Time: *10 minutes*

Quick Tip

For evenly cooked potatoes, be sure to choose potatoes that are about the same size.

Snowbird Mocktails

3 cups pineapple juice
1 can (14 ounces) sweetened condensed milk
1 can (6 ounces) frozen orange juice concentrate, thawed
½ teaspoon coconut extract
1 bottle (32 ounces) ginger ale, chilled

1. Combine pineapple juice, sweetened condensed milk, orange juice concentrate and coconut extract in large pitcher; stir well. Refrigerate, covered, up to 1 week.

2. To serve, pour ½ cup pineapple juice mixture into individual glasses (over crushed ice, if desired). Top off each glass with about ⅓ cup ginger ale. *Makes 10 servings*

Tip: Store unopened cans of sweetened condensed milk at room temperature up to 6 months. Once opened, store in airtight container in refrigerator for up to 5 days.

Chicken Nuggets Parmigiana

1 jar (26 to 28 ounces) RAGÚ® Old World Style® Pasta Sauce
1 package (12 ounces) refrigerated or frozen fully-cooked chicken nuggets (about 18 nuggets)
2 cups shredded mozzarella cheese (about 8 ounces)
1 tablespoon grated Parmesan cheese

1. Preheat oven to 375°F. In 13×9-inch baking dish, evenly spread 1½ cups Ragú Pasta Sauce. Arrange chicken nuggets in dish, top with remaining sauce and sprinkle with cheeses.

2. Cover with aluminum foil and bake 25 minutes. Remove foil and bake an additional 5 minutes. *Makes 4 to 6 servings*

Prep Time: *5 minutes*
Cook Time: *30 minutes*

Snowbird Mocktails

Main Dishes

Save time and energy—while making numerous fans—with one of these simple yet substantial main dish recipes. With a variety of cooking methods and a delightful mix of ingredients, you can serve up a different recipe every night. No one has to know that these great dishes are a snap to make!

Peppered Beef Rib Roast (recipe on page 27)

Oriental Beef Kabobs

1 tablespoon olive oil
1 tablespoon soy sauce
1 tablespoon seasoned rice vinegar
4 purchased beef kabobs

Preheat broiler. Position oven rack about 4 inches from heat source. Whisk together oil, soy sauce and vinegar; brush mixture on kabobs. Arrange kabobs on rack of broiler pan. Broil 10 minutes or to desired doneness, turning after 5 minutes. *Makes 4 servings*

Tuna & Noodles

2¼ cups water
3 cups (6 ounces) medium egg noodles, uncooked
¾ pound (12 ounces) VELVEETA® Pasteurized Prepared Cheese Product, cut up
1 package (16 ounces) frozen vegetable blend, thawed, drained
1 can (6 ounces) tuna, drained, flaked
¼ teaspoon black pepper

1. Bring water to boil in saucepan. Stir in noodles. Reduce heat to medium-low; cover. Simmer 8 minutes or until noodles are tender.

2. Add Velveeta, vegetables, tuna and pepper; stir until Velveeta is melted. *Makes 4 to 6 servings*

Take a Shortcut: When cooking pasta for Tuna & Noodles, you can double the amount you make and save half for a meal later in the week. Thoroughly drain the pasta you're not using, then put it in a bowl of ice water to stop the cooking. Drain thoroughly, then toss with 1 to 2 teaspoons of oil. Store in a zipper-style plastic bag in the refrigerator for up to 3 days.

Prep Time: *10 minutes*
Cook Time: *15 minutes*

Oriental Beef Kabobs

Fresco Marinated Chicken

Fresco Marinated Chicken

**1 envelope LIPTON® RECIPE SECRETS® Garlic Mushroom
   Soup Mix***
¹⁄₃ cup water
¹⁄₄ cup olive or vegetable oil
1 teaspoon lemon juice or vinegar
4 boneless, skinless chicken breast halves (about 1 ¹⁄₄ pounds)

**Also terrific with LIPTON® RECIPE SECRETS® Savory Herb with Garlic or Golden Onion Soup
Mix.*

1. For marinade, blend all ingredients except chicken.

2. In shallow baking dish or plastic bag, pour ½ cup of the marinade
over chicken. Cover, or close bag, and marinate in refrigerator, turning
occasionally, up to 3 hours. Refrigerate remaining marinade.

3. Remove chicken, discarding marinade. Grill or broil chicken,
turning once and brushing with refrigerated marinade until chicken is
no longer pink in center.   *Makes 4 servings*

Peppered Beef Rib Roast

1 ½ tablespoons black peppercorns
  1 boneless beef rib roast (2 ½ to 3 pounds), well trimmed
  ¼ cup Dijon mustard
  2 cloves garlic, minced
    Sour Cream Sauce (optional, page 64)

Prepare grill for indirect cooking.

Place peppercorns in small resealable plastic food storage bag. Squeeze out excess air; close bag securely. Pound peppercorns until cracked using flat side of meat mallet or rolling pin. Set aside.

Pat roast dry with paper towels. Combine mustard and garlic in small bowl; spread over top and sides of roast. Sprinkle pepper over mustard mixture.

Place roast, pepper-side up, on grid directly over drip pan. Grill, covered, over medium heat 1 hour to 1 hour 10 minutes for medium or until internal temperature reaches 145°F when tested with meat thermometer inserted into the thickest part of roast. Add 4 to 9 briquets to both sides of the fire after 45 minutes to maintain medium heat.

Meanwhile, prepare Sour Cream Sauce, if using. Cover; refrigerate until serving.

Transfer roast to cutting board; cover with foil. Let stand 10 to 15 minutes before carving. Internal temperature will continue to rise 5°F to 10°F during stand time. Serve with Sour Cream Sauce, if desired.

Makes 6 to 8 servings

Smart Tip

The indirect grilling method is used for slow cooking large roasts and whole chickens on the grill.

Peachy Pork Roast

1 (3- to 4-pound) rolled boneless pork loin roast
1 cup (12-ounce jar) SMUCKER'S® Currant Jelly
½ cup SMUCKER'S® Peach Preserves
Fresh peach slices and currants for garnish, if desired

Place pork in roasting pan; insert meat thermometer into one end of roast. Bake at 325°F for 30 to 40 minutes or until browned. Turn roast and bake an additional 30 minutes to brown the bottom. Turn roast again and drain off drippings.

In saucepan over medium heat, melt currant jelly and peach preserves. Brush roast generously with sauce.

Continue baking until meat thermometer reads 160°F, about 15 minutes, basting occasionally with sauce.

Remove roast from oven. Garnish with peach slices and currants. Serve with remaining sauce.   *Makes 8 to 10 servings*

Note: Canned, sliced peaches can be substituted for fresh peaches.

Saucy Chicken

2 pounds chicken breasts
1 (8-ounce) bottle Russian or French salad dressing
1 (1.25-ounce) envelope onion soup mix (dry)
1 cup (12-ounce jar) SMUCKER'S® Apricot Preserves
Hot cooked rice

Place chicken skin-side-up in 13×9-inch baking pan. Combine dressing, soup mix and preserves; mix well. Pour over chicken.

Bake at 350° for 1 hour or until chicken is fork-tender and juices run clear; halfway through cooking time, spoon sauce over breasts. Serve over hot cooked rice.   *Makes 8 servings*

Peachy Pork Roast

Herb Roasted Turkey

1 (12-pound) turkey, thawed if frozen
½ cup FLEISCHMANN'S® Original Margarine, softened, divided
1 tablespoon Italian seasoning

1. Remove neck and giblets from turkey cavities. Rinse turkey; drain well and pat dry. Free legs from tucked position; do not cut band of skin. Using rubber spatula or hand, loosen skin over breast, starting at body cavity opening by legs.

2. Blend 6 tablespoons margarine and Italian seasoning. Spread 2 tablespoons herb mixture inside body cavity; spread remaining herb mixture on meat under skin. Hold skin in place at opening with wooden picks. Return legs to tucked position; turn wings back to hold neck skin in place.

3. Place turkey, breast-side up, on flat rack in shallow open pan. Insert meat thermometer deep into thickest part of thigh next to body, not touching bone. Melt remaining 2 tablespoons margarine; brush over skin.

4. Roast at 325°F for 3½ to 3¾ hours. When skin is golden brown, shield breast loosely with foil to prevent overbrowning. Check for doneness; thigh temperature should be 180°F to 185°F. Transfer turkey to cutting board; let stand 15 to 20 minutes before carving. Remove wooden toothpicks just before carving.   *Makes 12 servings*

Prep Time: *20 minutes*
Cook Time: *3 hours and 30 minutes*
Cooling Time: *15 minutes*
Total Time: *4 hours and 5 minutes*

Herb Roasted Turkey

Eggstra Special Omelets for Two

6 eggs
3 tablespoons half and half, light cream or milk
¼ teaspoon salt
⅛ teaspoon ground black pepper
2 tablespoons I CAN'T BELIEVE IT'S NOT BUTTER!® Spread, divided
Special Omelet Fillings

In small bowl, with wire whisk or fork, beat eggs, half and half, salt and pepper; set aside.

In 8-inch nonstick skillet, melt 1 tablespoon I Can't Believe It's Not Butter! Spread and add ½ of the egg mixture. With spatula, lift set edges of omelet, tilting pan to allow uncooked mixture to flow to bottom. When omelet is set and slightly moist, add desired Special Omelet Filling. With spatula, fold omelet and cook an additional 30 seconds. Repeat with remaining 1 tablespoon I Can't Believe It's Not Butter! Spread and egg mixture.   *Makes 2 servings*

Special Omelet Fillings:
Springtime Asparagus Omelet: In 10-inch skillet, melt 2 tablespoons I CAN'T BELIEVE IT'S NOT BUTTER!® Spread over medium-high heat and cook ¼ cup chopped shallots or onions until tender. Add 1½ cups cut-up asparagus and salt and ground black pepper to taste. Cook until asparagus is tender. Spoon into omelets, then evenly sprinkle with ¼ cup grated Parmesan cheese.

Western Omelet: In 10-inch skillet, melt 1 tablespoon I CAN'T BELIEVE IT'S NOT BUTTER!® Spread over medium-high heat and cook 1 cup chopped bell pepper, 1 cup diced potatoes, ½ cup chopped onion and salt and ground black pepper to taste, stirring occasionally, until vegetables are tender. Spoon into omelets.

Florentine Omelet: In 10-inch skillet, melt 2 tablespoons I CAN'T BELIEVE IT'S NOT BUTTER!® Spread over medium-high heat and cook ¼ cup chopped shallots or onions until tender. Add 4 cups baby spinach leaves and cook, stirring occasionally, until wilted. Stir in

Eggstra Special Omelet for Two

½ cup chopped prosciutto (optional) and ground black pepper to taste. Spoon into omelets, then evenly sprinkle, if desired, with ½ cup crumbled goat cheese.

Salmon Omelet: Fill omelets with 2 thin slices smoked salmon, 2 tablespoons chopped red onion, 2 teaspoons chopped drained capers, ¼ cup cream cheese and salt and ground black pepper to taste.

Fresh Tomato-Basil Omelet: Fill omelets with 2 chopped plum tomatoes, ⅔ cup chopped fresh mozzarella cheese, 4 fresh basil leaves, cut into thin strips and salt and ground black pepper to taste.

Fiesta Omelet: In 10-inch skillet, melt 2 tablespoons I CAN'T BELIEVE IT'S NOT BUTTER!® Spread over medium-high heat and cook ½ cup chopped onion until tender. Add 1 cup drained canned black beans, ¼ cup chopped green chilies and salt and ground black pepper to taste; heat through. Spoon into omelets, then evenly sprinkle with 1 cup shredded Monterey Jack or Monterey Jack cheese with jalapeño peppers (about 4 ounces).

Jamaican Shrimp & Pineapple Kabobs

½ cup prepared jerk sauce
¼ cup pineapple preserves
2 tablespoons minced fresh chives
1 pound large shrimp, peeled and deveined
½ medium pineapple, peeled, cored and cut into 1-inch cubes
2 large red, green or yellow bell peppers, cut into 1-inch squares

1. Combine jerk sauce, preserves and chives in small bowl; mix well. Thread shrimp, pineapple and peppers onto 4 skewers; brush with jerk sauce mixture.

2. Grill kabobs over medium-hot coals 6 to 10 minutes or until shrimp turn pink and opaque, turning once. Serve with remaining jerk sauce mixture. *Makes 4 servings*

Prep and Cook Time: *25 minutes*

Campbell's® Lemon Asparagus Chicken

1 tablespoon vegetable oil
4 skinless, boneless chicken breast halves (about 1 pound)
1 can (10¾ ounces) CAMPBELL'S® Condensed Cream of Asparagus Soup
¼ cup milk
1 tablespoon lemon juice
⅛ teaspoon pepper

1. In medium skillet over medium-high heat, heat oil. Add chicken and cook 8 minutes or until browned. Set chicken aside. Pour off fat.

2. Add soup, milk, lemon juice and pepper. Heat to a boil. Return chicken to pan. Reduce heat to low. Cover and cook 5 minutes or until chicken is no longer pink. *Makes 4 servings*

Prep/Cook Time: *20 minutes*

Jamaican Shrimp & Pineapple Kabobs

Sweet and Sour Pork

³/₄ pound boneless pork
1 teaspoon vegetable oil
1 bag (16 ounces) BIRDS EYE® frozen Farm Fresh Mixtures
   Pepper Stir Fry vegetables
1 tablespoon water
1 jar (14 ounces) sweet and sour sauce
1 can (8 ounces) pineapple chunks, drained

• Cut pork into thin strips.

• In large skillet, heat oil over medium-high heat.

• Add pork; stir-fry until pork is browned.

• Add vegetables and water; cover and cook over medium heat 5 to 7 minutes or until vegetables are crisp-tender.

• Uncover; stir in sweet and sour sauce and pineapple. Cook until heated through.   *Makes 4 servings*

Serving Suggestion: Serve over hot cooked rice.

Prep Time: *5 minutes*
Cook Time: *15 to 18 minutes*

Quick Tip

For a quick sweet and sour sauce for chicken nuggets or egg rolls, add sugar and vinegar to taste to jarred strained apricots or peaches.

Sweet and Sour Pork

Roast Turkey with Honey Cranberry Relish

Roast Turkey with Honey Cranberry Relish

  1 medium orange
12 ounces fresh or frozen whole cranberries
¾ cup honey
  2 pounds sliced roasted turkey breast

Quarter and slice unpeeled orange, removing seeds. Coarsely chop orange and cranberries. Place in medium saucepan and stir in honey. Bring to a boil over medium-high heat. Cook 3 to 4 minutes; cool. Serve over turkey.   *Makes 8 servings*

Favorite recipe from **National Honey Board**

Cheese-Stuffed Meat Loaf

1 ½ **pounds ground beef**
  1 **jar (26 to 28 ounces) RAGÚ® Chunky Gardenstyle Pasta Sauce**
  1 **large egg, slightly beaten**
  ¼ **cup plain dry bread crumbs**
  2 **cups shredded mozzarella cheese (about 8 ounces)**
  1 **tablespoon finely chopped fresh parsley**

1. Preheat oven to 350°F. In large bowl, combine ground beef, ⅓ cup Ragú Pasta Sauce, egg and bread crumbs. Season, if desired, with salt and ground black pepper. In 13×9-inch baking or roasting pan, shape into 12×8-inch rectangle.

2. Sprinkle 1½ cups cheese and parsley down center leaving ¾-inch border. Roll, starting at long end, jelly-roll style. Press ends together to seal.

3. Bake uncovered 45 minutes. Pour remaining sauce over meat loaf and sprinkle with remaining ½ cup cheese. Bake an additional 15 minutes or until sauce is heated through and cheese is melted. Let stand 5 minutes before serving. *Makes 6 servings*

Tip: Molding the meat mixture onto waxed paper helps make rolling easier. Just lift waxed paper to curl the meat over cheese filling, then carefully remove meat from paper. Continue rolling in this manner until filling is enclosed in roll and meat is off paper.

Prep Time: *20 minutes*
Cook Time: 1 *hour*

Scallops with Tomatoes and Basil

8 to 12 large sea scallops, halved crosswise
Salt and freshly ground black pepper, to taste
3 tablespoons FLEISCHMANN'S® Original Margarine, divided
2 tomatoes, peeled, seeded and chopped
2 tablespoons chopped fresh or 2 teaspoons dried basil
leaves

1. Dry scallops with paper towels; season with salt and pepper.

2. Heat 2 tablespoons margarine in large nonstick skillet over medium-high heat.

3. Arrange half the scallops in a single layer in skillet; cook for 1 to 2 minutes on each side or just until cooked. Transfer scallops to a platter; keep warm. Repeat with remaining scallops; remove to serving platter.

4. Melt remaining margarine in same skillet over medium-high heat. Add tomatoes and basil; heat through.

5. Spoon tomato mixture over the scallops; serve immediately.

Makes 2 servings

Prep Time: *10 minutes*
Cook Time: *5 minutes*
Total Time: *15 minutes*

Scallops with Tomatoes and Basil

Crispy Onion Chicken Fingers

Crispy Onion Chicken Fingers

1 ⅓ cups *French's*® *Taste Toppers*™ French Fried Onions
1 pound boneless skinless chicken fingers
3 to 4 tablespoons *French's*® Honey Mustard

1. Preheat oven to 400°F. Place **Taste Toppers** in resealable plastic food storage bag; seal. Crush **Taste Toppers** with rolling pin.

2. Coat chicken fingers with mustard. Dip into crushed **Taste Toppers**. Place chicken on baking sheet.

3. Bake 15 minutes or until chicken is crispy and no longer pink in center.   *Makes 4 servings*

Prep Time: *10 minutes*
Cook Time: *15 minutes*

Steak & Pepper Fajitas

1 packet (1.12 ounces) fajita marinade
1 pound boneless steak,* cut into thin strips
1 bag (16 ounces) BIRDS EYE® frozen Farm Fresh Mixtures
    Pepper Stir Fry vegetables
8 (6- to 7-inch) flour tortillas, warmed
½ cup salsa

*Or, substitute 1 pound boneless, skinless chicken, cut into strips.

• Prepare fajita marinade according to package directions.

• Add steak and vegetables. Let stand 10 minutes.

• Heat large skillet over medium-high heat. Remove steak and vegetables with slotted spoon and place in skillet.

• Add marinade, if desired. Cook 5 minutes or until steak is desired doneness and mixture is heated through, stirring occasionally.

• Wrap mixture in tortillas. Top with salsa.   *Makes 4 servings*

Birds Eye Idea: Vegetables do not have to be fresh to be nutritious. Add cooked Birds Eye® broccoli or spinach to frozen pizza.

Prep Time: *10 minutes*
Cook Time: *5 to 7 minutes*

Serving Tip

*Serve these zesty fajitas with guacamole and sour cream
on the side. Or, serve the beef and vegetable mixture over
rice if you don't have tortillas on hand.*

Sides and Salads

Once you've created a tantalizing meal in minutes, why not enhance it with a healthful side dish or an attractive salad? When teamed up with these sure-fire dishes, the centerpiece of your meal will reach heavenly heights...with minimal effort.

Create your own favorite meal combinations.

Grilled Chicken Caesar Salad (recipe on page 48)

Easy Veggie-Topped Baked Spuds

2½ cups frozen broccoli-carrot vegetable medley
4 large baking potatoes
1 can (10¾ ounces) cream of broccoli soup
½ cup (2 ounces) shredded Cheddar cheese
Salt and pepper

1. Place vegetables in microwavable bowl. Microwave at HIGH
5 minutes; drain.

2. Scrub potatoes; pierce several times with knife. Microwave at HIGH
15 minutes or until potatoes are soft.

3. While potatoes are cooking, combine soup, vegetables and cheese
in medium saucepan. Cook and stir over low heat until cheese melts
and mixture is heated through.

4. Split baked potatoes in half. Top each potato with soup mixture.
Season to taste with salt and pepper.   *Makes 4 servings*

Prep and Cook Time: *23 minutes*

Smart Tip

*Choose russet or Idaho potatoes for baking. Store them in
a cool, dark place away from onions for up to 2 weeks.
(Storing potatoes and onions together will cause the
potatoes to rot more quickly.)*

Easy Veggie-Topped Baked Spuds

Spinach-Orange Salad

 1 large bunch spinach, stems removed
 2 oranges
 ½ small jicama, peeled and cut into julienne strips (about
     1 cup)
 ¼ cup toasted pecan halves
     Prepared vinaigrette dressing

Wash and dry spinach; chill until very crisp. Tear into bite-size pieces; place in large bowl. Peel oranges, removing white membrane. Cut segments between membranes to remove; chop. Add oranges, jicama and pecans to spinach. Pour vinaigrette dressing over spinach mixture and toss gently until well mixed.   *Makes 6 servings*

Grilled Chicken Caesar Salad

 8 cups torn romaine lettuce
 1 pound boneless skinless chicken breasts, grilled, cut into
     strips
 1 cup seasoned croutons
 ½ cup KRAFT® Shredded or 100% Grated Parmesan Cheese
 ¾ cup KRAFT FREE® Caesar Italian Fat Free Dressing

TOSS lettuce, chicken, croutons and cheese in large salad bowl.

ADD dressing; toss to coat. Serve with fresh lemon wedges and fresh ground pepper, if desired.   *Makes 4 servings*

Variation: Prepare as directed, substituting 1 package (10 ounces) mixed or romaine salad greens.

Prep Time: *15 minutes plus marinating*
Grill Time: *20 minutes*

Spinach-Orange Salad

Grilled Corn-on-the-Cob

Grilled Corn-on-the-Cob

¼ pound butter or margarine, softened
1 tablespoon KIKKOMAN® Soy Sauce
½ teaspoon dried tarragon leaves, crumbled
6 ears fresh corn

Thoroughly blend butter, soy sauce and tarragon leaves. Husk corn. Lay each ear on piece of foil large enough to wrap around it; spread ears generously with seasoned butter. Wrap foil around corn; seal edges. Place on grill 3 inches from hot coals; cook 20 to 30 minutes, or until corn is tender, turning over frequently. (Or, place wrapped corn on baking sheet. Bake in 325°F oven 30 minutes.) Serve immediately.   *Makes 6 servings*

Note: Butter-soy mixture may also be spread on hot boiled corn.

Broccoli and Onion Casserole

    1 large onion
    ¾ cup fat-free low-sodium chicken broth*
    1¼ pounds broccoli
    ½ teaspoon black pepper, divided
       Dash paprika

Preheat oven to 375°F. Cut onion into quarters, then crosswise into thin slices. Bring onion and chicken broth to a boil in medium saucepan over high heat. Reduce heat to low. Simmer, covered, 5 minutes or until onion is fork-tender. Remove onion to small bowl with slotted spoon, leaving broth in saucepan. Set aside.

Trim broccoli, removing tough part of stems. Cut into florets with ½-inch stems. Peel remaining broccoli stems; cut into ¼-inch-thick slices.

Spread half of broccoli in 8-inch square baking dish or 2-quart casserole. Spread half of onion slices on broccoli. Sprinkle with ¼ teaspoon pepper. Repeat layers.

Pour reserved broth over vegetables. Cover tightly with foil. Bake 25 minutes or until broccoli is tender. *Do not stir.* Drain liquid; sprinkle with paprika before serving.   *Makes 6 servings*

Pineapple Yam Casserole

    4 medium yams, cooked, peeled and mashed, *or* 2 (16- or
       17-ounce) cans yams, drained and mashed
    ⅓ cup SMUCKER'S® Pineapple Topping
    4 tablespoons butter or margarine, melted, divided
    1 tablespoon lemon juice

Combine yams, pineapple topping, 3 tablespoons butter and lemon juice; mix well. Brush 1-quart casserole with remaining 1 tablespoon butter. Spoon yam mixture into casserole.

Bake at 350°F for 25 minutes or until heated through.

                                                    Makes 4 servings

Carpaccio di Zucchini

¾ pound zucchini, shredded
½ cup sliced almonds, toasted
1 tablespoon prepared Italian dressing
4 French bread baguettes, sliced in half lengthwise
4 teaspoons soft spread margarine
3 tablespoons grated Parmesan cheese

1. Preheat broiler. Place zucchini in medium bowl. Add almonds and dressing; mix well. Set aside.

2. Place baguette halves on large baking sheet; spread evenly with margarine. Sprinkle with cheese. Broil 3 inches from heat 2 to 3 minutes or until edges and cheese are browned.

3. Spread zucchini mixture evenly on each baguette half. Serve immediately. *Makes 4 servings*

Go-with suggestions: Spaghetti with tomato sauce.

Prep and Cook Time: *28 minutes*

Lemon Basil Broccoli

1 bag (16 ounces) BIRDS EYE® frozen Broccoli Cuts
2 tablespoons butter, melted
¼ teaspoon lemon juice
¼ teaspoon dried basil

• Cook broccoli according to package directions; drain.

• Combine butter, lemon juice and basil in small bowl; mix well.

• Combine broccoli and butter mixture; toss to blend.

Makes 4 servings

Prep Time: *2 minutes*
Cook Time: *8 minutes*

Carpaccio di Zucchini

Roasted Potato and Vegetable Salad

2 pounds red potatoes, cubed
2 zucchini, thinly sliced lengthwise
2 carrots, diagonally sliced
1 small red onion, cut into wedges
2 cups KRAFT® TASTE OF LIFE™ Tomato & Garlic Dressing

TOSS vegetables with dressing in large bowl.

SPOON into shallow roasting pan.

BAKE at 400°F for 40 to 45 minutes or until vegetables are tender, stirring occasionally.

Makes 8 servings

Prep Time: 10 *minutes*
Bake Time: 45 *minutes*

Holiday Vegetable Bake

1 package (16 ounces) frozen vegetable combination
1 can (10¾ ounces) condensed cream of broccoli soup
⅓ cup milk
1⅓ cups French's® Taste Toppers™ French Fried Onions, divided

Microwave Directions:
Combine vegetables, soup, milk and ⅔ *cup* **Taste Toppers** in 2-quart microwavable casserole. Microwave,* uncovered, on HIGH 10 to 12 minutes or until vegetables are crisp-tender, stirring halfway through cooking time. Sprinkle with remaining ⅔ *cup* **Taste Toppers**. Microwave 1 minute or until **Taste Toppers** are golden.

Makes 4 to 6 servings

*Or, bake in preheated 375°F oven 30 to 35 minutes.

Prep Time: 5 *minutes*
Cook Time: 10 *minutes*

Roasted Potato and Vegetable Salad

Broth-Braised Brussels Sprouts

1 pound fresh Brussels sprouts
½ cup condensed beef broth *or* ½ cup water plus 2 teaspoons
    instant beef bouillon granules
1 tablespoon butter or margarine, softened
¼ cup freshly grated Parmesan cheese
    Paprika

1. Trim stems from Brussels sprouts and pull off outer discolored leaves.

2. Use large enough saucepan to allow sprouts to fit in single layer. Place sprouts and broth in saucepan. Bring to a boil; reduce heat. Cover; simmer about 5 minutes or just until sprouts turn bright green and are crisp-tender.

3. Uncover; simmer until liquid is almost evaporated. Toss cooked sprouts with butter, then cheese. Sprinkle with paprika to taste. Garnish as desired.   *Makes 4 servings*

Tip: For faster, more even cooking, cut an "X" deep into the stem end of each Brussels sprout.

Vegetable Stir-Fry

1 tablespoon vegetable oil
3 to 4 carrots, diagonally sliced
2 zucchini, diagonally sliced
3 tablespoons orange juice
    Salt and pepper

Heat oil in medium skillet or wok over medium heat. Add carrots; stir-fry 3 minutes. Add zucchini and orange juice; stir-fry 4 minutes or until vegetables are crisp-tender. Season with salt and pepper to taste.   *Makes 4 servings*

Broth-Braised Brussels Sprouts

Cole Slaw Vinaigrette

  ¼ **cup vegetable oil**
  2 **tablespoons white wine vinegar**
  1 **tablespoon honey**
    Salt and pepper
  1 **(8-ounce) package cole slaw mix**

Whisk together oil, vinegar and honey. Season with salt and pepper to taste. Place cole slaw mix in medium bowl. Pour vinaigrette over cole slaw mix. Toss lightly to coat; cover. Refrigerate.   *Makes 4 servings*

Nutty Vegetable Duo

  1 **(10-ounce) package frozen green beans**
  ½ **(16-ounce) package frozen small whole onions**
  ¼ **cup toasted slivered almonds**
  2 **tablespoons butter or margarine**
    Salt and black pepper

1. Combine beans and onions in medium saucepan; cook according to package directions. Drain.

2. Return vegetables to saucepan. Add almonds and butter; stir over low heat until butter is melted and mixture is thoroughly heated. Season with salt and pepper to taste.   *Makes 4 servings*

Smart Tip

To toast almonds, spread them evenly in shallow baking pan. Bake at 350°F, 8 to 10 minutes or until lightly toasted, stirring occasionally.

Warm Steak Salad

Warm Steak Salad

1 beef flank steak (about 1 ¼ pounds)
Salt and pepper
¼ pound sugar snap peas or snow peas
Lettuce leaves
1 medium red onion, sliced, separated into rings
1 pint cherry tomatoes
Prepared honey mustard dressing (optional)

1. Preheat broiler. Position oven rack about 4 inches from heat source.

2. Place steak on rack of broiler pan. Broil 10 minutes or to desired doneness, turning after 5 minutes. Season with salt and pepper to taste.

3. Meanwhile, bring lightly salted water to a boil in medium saucepan. Add peas; cook 2 minutes. Drain.

4. Place steak on cutting board. Cut diagonally across grain of meat into thin slices.

5. Line serving platter with lettuce. Arrange steak slices in center of platter. Surround with onion rings, snow peas and cherry tomatoes. Serve with prepared honey mustard dressing, if desired.

Makes 4 servings

Marinades and Sauces

Complement a good piece of poultry, meat

or fish with a flavorful marinade or sauce that adds

the final touch and brings out its full flavor. Simple

fruits and other desserts become temptations beyond

compare when embellished with a splendid sweet

sauce. Just the touch to take a meal from

pretty good to perfect.

Sweet 'n' Smoky BBQ Sauce (recipe on page 71)

Basil Mayonnaise

½ cup mayonnaise
½ cup sour cream or plain yogurt
1 green onion, cut into 1-inch pieces
2 tablespoons fresh parsley
2 tablespoons fresh basil
Salt and pepper

Combine mayonnaise, sour cream, onion, parsley and basil in food processor or blender; process until well blended. Season with salt and pepper to taste.   *Makes about 1¼ cups*

Mustard Vinaigrette

2 tablespoons country-style Dijon mustard
½ cup seasoned rice vinegar
¼ cup vegetable oil
½ teaspoon dark sesame oil
Dash black pepper

Whisk together all ingredients in small bowl.   *Makes about ¾ cup*

Quick Tip

To make a tossed salad ahead, place the firm vegetables and meat or poultry in the bottom of the salad bowl and add the salad dressing. Top with the salad greens but do not toss. Refrigerate the mixture for up to 2 hours. Toss the salad just before serving.

Mustard Vinaigrette

Fresh Fruit Sauce

½ cup KARO® Light Corn Syrup
2 cups fresh berries, chopped kiwifruit or chopped peaches
1 teaspoon lemon juice
¼ teaspoon almond extract *or* ½ cup chopped fresh fruit

1. In blender or food processor combine corn syrup, 2 cups fruit and lemon juice. Process until smooth.

2. Stir in almond extract or chopped fresh fruit.　　*Makes about 2 cups*

Strawberry Sauce

1 pint strawberries, hulled
2 to 3 tablespoons sugar
1 tablespoon strawberry- or orange-flavored liqueur (optional)

Combine strawberries, sugar and liqueur in blender or food processor. Cover; process until smooth.　　*Makes 1½ cups*

Sour Cream Sauce

¾ cup sour cream
2 tablespoons prepared horseradish
1 tablespoon balsamic vinegar
½ teaspoon sugar

Combine all ingredients in small bowl; mix well.　　*Makes about 1 cup*

Fresh Fruit Sauce

Onion Wine Sauce

4 cups onion wedges
2 cloves garlic, minced
2 tablespoons margarine or butter
½ cup A.1.® Original or A.1.® BOLD & SPICY Steak Sauce
2 tablespoons red cooking wine

In large skillet, over medium-high heat, cook and stir onions and garlic in margarine until tender, about 10 minutes. Stir in steak sauce and wine; heat to a boil. Reduce heat; simmer 5 minutes. Serve hot with cooked steak.   *Makes 2½ cups*

Easy Tartar Sauce

¼ cup fat-free or reduced-fat mayonnaise
2 tablespoons sweet pickle relish
1 teaspoon lemon juice

Combine mayonnaise, relish and lemon juice in small bowl; mix well. Refrigerate until ready to serve.   *Makes about ¼ cup*

Lemon Pepper Marinade

⅔ cup A.1.® Steak Sauce
4 teaspoons grated lemon peel
1½ teaspoons coarsely ground black pepper

In small nonmetal bowl, combine steak sauce, lemon peel and pepper. Use to marinate beef, fish, steak, poultry or pork for about 1 hour in the refrigerator.   *Makes about ⅔ cup*

Onion Wine Sauce

Ever-So-Good Peanut Butter Sauce

½ cup KARO® Light or Dark Corn Syrup
½ cup SKIPPY® SUPER CHUNK® or Creamy Peanut Butter
3 to 4 tablespoons milk

1. In small bowl stir corn syrup, peanut butter and milk until blended.

2. Serve over ice cream or cake. Store in refrigerator.

Makes about 1¼ cups

Prep Time: *5 minutes*

Hot Chocolate Fudge Sauce

¾ cup sugar
¾ cup heavy or whipping cream
½ cup KARO® Light Corn Syrup
2 tablespoons margarine or butter
1 package (8 ounces) semisweet chocolate
1 teaspoon vanilla

1. In large saucepan combine sugar, cream, corn syrup and margarine. Stirring constantly, bring to full boil over medium heat. Remove from heat.

2. Stir in chocolate until melted. Stir in vanilla.

3. Serve warm over ice cream. Store in refrigerator.

Makes about 2¼ cups

Prep Time: *10 minutes, plus cooling*

Clockwise from top: Hot Chocolate Fudge Sauce, Ever-So-Good Peanut Butter Sauce and Maple Walnut Raisin Sauce (recipe on page 71)

Zippy Tartar Sauce for Grilled Fish

Zippy Tartar Sauce for Grilled Fish

1 cup mayonnaise
3 tablespoons Frank's® RedHot® Sauce
2 tablespoons French's® Hearty Deli Brown Mustard
2 tablespoons sweet pickle relish
1 tablespoon minced capers

Combine mayonnaise, **RedHot** Sauce, mustard, pickle relish and capers in medium bowl. Cover and chill in refrigerator until ready to serve. Serve with grilled salmon, halibut, swordfish or tuna.

Makes 1 ½ cups

Prep Time: *5 minutes*

Maple Walnut Raisin Sauce

1 cup KARO® Light or Dark Corn Syrup
1/2 cup packed brown sugar
1/2 cup heavy or whipping cream
1/2 cup coarsely chopped walnuts
1/4 cup raisins
1/2 teaspoon maple-flavored extract

1. In medium saucepan combine corn syrup, brown sugar and cream. Stirring constantly, bring to full boil over medium heat and boil 1 minute. Remove from heat.

2. Stir in walnuts, raisins and maple extract. Serve warm. Store in refrigerator.   *Makes 2 cups*

Prep Time: *10 minutes*

Sweet 'n' Smoky BBQ Sauce

1/2 cup ketchup
1/3 cup French's® Hearty Deli Brown Mustard
1/3 cup light molasses
1/4 cup French's® Worcestershire Sauce
1/4 teaspoon liquid smoke or hickory salt (optional)

Combine ketchup, mustard, molasses, Worcestershire and liquid smoke, if desired, in medium bowl. Mix until well blended. Brush on chicken or ribs during last 15 minutes of grilling.

Makes about 1 1/2 cups

Prep Time: *5 minutes*

Desserts and Treats

Beautiful desserts are always special additions to a great meal. Cool, fresh sensations are a great way to round out a summer lunch. Or, top a delicately layered treat with warm sauce to finish a tremendous winter supper. Any of these dazzling and easy-to-make delights will have everyone asking for more.

Light Banana Cream Pie (recipe on page 75)

Chocolate Macadamia Chippers

Chocolate Macadamia Chippers

**1 package (18 ounces) refrigerated chocolate chip cookie
dough**
3 tablespoons unsweetened cocoa powder
$\frac{1}{2}$ cup coarsely chopped macadamia nuts

Preheat oven to 375°F. Remove dough from wrapper.

Place dough in medium bowl; stir in cocoa until well blended. (Dough
may be kneaded lightly, if desired.) Stir in nuts. Drop by rounded
tablespoonfuls 2 inches apart onto ungreased cookie sheets.

Bake 9 to 11 minutes or until almost set. Transfer to wire racks to cool
completely.   *Makes 2 dozen cookies*

Light Banana Cream Pie

**1 package (1.9 ounces) sugar-free vanilla instant pudding and
pie filling (4 servings)**
2¾ cups low fat milk
4 ripe, medium DOLE® Bananas, sliced
1 (9-inch) ready-made graham cracker pie crust
1 firm, medium DOLE® Banana (optional)
Light frozen non-dairy whipped topping, thawed (optional)

• **Prepare** pudding as directed using 2¾ cups low fat milk. Stir in
4 sliced ripe bananas.

• **Spoon** banana mixture into pie crust. Place plastic wrap over pie,
lightly pressing plastic to completely cover filling. Chill 1 hour or until
filling is set. Remove plastic wrap.

• **Cut** firm banana into ½-inch slices. Garnish pie with whipped
topping and banana slices. *Makes 8 servings*

Prep time: *10 minutes*
Chill time: *1 hour*

Strawberry Hearts

1 roll (17 to 18 ounces) refrigerated sugar cookie dough
2 packages (8 ounces *each*) cream cheese, softened
⅔ cup powdered sugar
1 teaspoon vanilla extract
2 cups sliced fresh strawberries

Roll out dough, cut out hearts and bake as directed on package.

Combine cream cheese, sugar and vanilla; mix well.

Spread evenly onto cooled hearts; top with strawberries.
Makes about 2 dozen hearts

Englishman's Trifle

1 box (10 ounces) BIRDS EYE® frozen Strawberries*
1 package (3.4 ounces) vanilla instant pudding
1 ½ cups milk
1 cup thawed frozen whipped topping
8 thin slices fresh or thawed frozen pound cake
½ cup toasted sliced almonds
¼ cup mini semisweet chocolate chips (optional)

Or, substitute Birds Eye® frozen Raspberries.

• Thaw strawberries according to package directions.

• Prepare pudding with 1 ½ cups milk according to package directions. Let stand 5 minutes; gently stir in whipped topping.

• Place 1 slice cake in each of 4 individual serving bowls. Spoon half the strawberries over cake. Top with half the pudding mixture, almonds and chocolate chips.

• Repeat layers of cake, strawberries, pudding, almonds and chips. Cover and chill until ready to serve.   *Makes 4 servings*

Prep Time: *20 minutes*

Englishman's Trifle

Chocolate Plunge

⅔ cup KARO® Light or Dark Corn Syrup
½ cup heavy cream
  8 squares (1 ounce each) semisweet chocolate
  Assorted fresh fruit

1. In medium saucepan combine corn syrup and cream. Bring to a boil over medium heat. Remove from heat.

2. Add chocolate; stir until completely melted.

3. Serve warm as a dip for fruit.   *Makes 1½ cups*

Try some of these "dippers": Candied pineapple, dried apricots, waffle squares, ladyfingers, cubed pound cake, macaroons, pretzels, croissants, mint cookies or peanut butter cookies.

Chocolate Plunge can be made a day ahead. Store covered in refrigerator. Reheat before serving.

Microwave Plunge: In medium microwavable bowl, combine corn syrup and cream. Microwave at HIGH 1½ minutes or until boiling. Add chocolate; stir until completely melted. Serve as directed.

Prep Time: *10 minutes*

Quick Tip

Check out the cut-up fresh fruit in your supermarket salad bar for a no-fuss way to "prepare" fruit for last-minute desserts. Add a festive touch with a variety of colors, shapes and textures.

Chocolate Plunge

Strawberry Miracle Mold

1 ½ **cups boiling water**
  2 **packages (4-serving size) JELL-O® Brand Strawberry Flavor Gelatin**
1 ¾ **cups cold water**
  ½ **cup MIRACLE WHIP® Salad Dressing**
  Assorted fruit

Stir boiling water into gelatin in medium bowl 2 minutes or until dissolved. Stir in cold water. Gradually whisk gelatin into salad dressing in large bowl until well blended.

Pour into 1-quart mold or glass serving bowl that has been lightly sprayed with no-stick cooking spray. Refrigerate until firm. Unmold onto serving plate; serve with fruit.   *Makes 4 to 6 servings*

Prep Time: *10 minutes plus refrigerating*

Cherry-Topped Lemon Cheesecake Pie

  1 **(8-ounce) package cream cheese, softened**
  1 **(14-ounce) can EAGLE® BRAND Sweetened Condensed Milk (NOT evaporated milk)**
⅓ **cup REALEMON® Lemon Juice From Concentrate**
  1 **teaspoon vanilla extract**
  1 **(6-ounce) ready-made graham cracker crumb pie crust**
  1 **(21-ounce) can cherry pie filling, chilled**

1. In large bowl, beat cream cheese until fluffy. Gradually beat in **Eagle Brand** until smooth. Stir in **ReaLemon** and vanilla. Pour into crust. Chill at least 3 hours.

2. To serve, top with cherry pie filling. Store covered in refrigerator.
                                     Makes 6 to 8 servings

Prep Time: *10 minutes*
Chill Time: *3 hours*

Luscious Lime Angel Food Cake Rolls

Luscious Lime Angel Food Cake Rolls

1 package (16 ounces) angel food cake mix
2 drops green food coloring (optional)
2 containers (8 ounces each) lime-flavored nonfat sugar-free yogurt
Lime slices (optional)

1. Preheat oven to 350°F. Line two 17×11¼×1-inch jelly-roll pans with parchment or waxed paper; set aside.

2. Prepare angel food cake mix according to package directions. Divide batter evenly between prepared pans. Draw knife through batter to remove large air bubbles. Bake 12 minutes or until cakes are lightly browned and toothpick inserted in centers comes out clean.

3. Invert each cake onto separate clean towel. Starting at short end, roll up warm cake, jelly-roll fashion, with towel inside. Cool cakes completely.

4. Place 1 to 2 drops green food coloring in each container of yogurt, if desired; stir well. Unroll cake; remove towel. Spread each cake with 1 container yogurt, leaving 1-inch border. Roll up cake; place seam-side-down. Slice each cake roll into 8 pieces. Garnish with lime slices, if desired. Serve immediately or refrigerate. *Makes 16 servings*

Mimosa Mold

1 ½ cups boiling water
   1 package (8-serving size) *or* 2 packages (4-serving size)
      JELL-O® Brand Sparkling White Grape or Lemon Flavor
      Gelatin Dessert
   2 cups cold seltzer or club soda
   1 can (11 ounces) mandarin orange segments, drained
   1 cup sliced strawberries

STIR boiling water into gelatin in large bowl at least 2 minutes or until completely dissolved. Refrigerate 15 minutes. Gently stir in seltzer. Refrigerate about 30 minutes or until slightly thickened (consistency of unbeaten egg whites). Gently stir about 15 seconds. Stir in oranges and strawberries. Pour into 6-cup mold.

REFRIGERATE 4 hours or until firm. Unmold. Garnish as desired. Store leftover gelatin mold in refrigerator.   *Makes 12 servings*

Preparation Time: *15 minutes*
Refrigerating Time: *4¾ hours*

Smart Tip

To unmold, dip mold in warm water for about 15 seconds. Gently pull gelatin from around edges with moist fingers. Place moistened serving plate on top of mold. Invert mold and plate; holding mold and plate together, shake slightly to loosen. Gently remove mold and center gelatin on plate.

Mimosa Mold

Angel Almond Cupcakes

1 package DUNCAN HINES® Angel Food Cake Mix
1 1/4 cups water
2 teaspoons almond extract
1 container DUNCAN HINES® Wild Cherry Vanilla Frosting

Preheat oven to 350°F.

Combine cake mix, water and almond extract in large mixing bowl. Beat at low speed with electric mixer until moistened. Beat at medium speed for 1 minute. Line medium muffin pans with paper baking cups. Fill muffin cups two-thirds full. Bake 20 to 25 minutes or until golden brown, cracked and dry. Remove from muffin pans. Cool completely. Frost with frosting.   *Makes 30 to 32 cupcakes*

Nutty Lemon Crescents

1 package (18 ounces) refrigerated sugar cookie dough
1 cup chopped pecans, toasted*
1 tablespoon grated lemon peel
1 1/2 cups powdered sugar, divided

*To toast pecans, spread in single layer on baking sheet. Bake in preheated 350°F oven 8 to 10 minutes or until golden brown, stirring frequently.

1. Preheat oven to 375°F. Remove dough from wrapper according to package directions.

2. Combine dough, pecans and lemon peel in large bowl. Stir until thoroughly blended. Shape level tablespoonfuls of dough into crescent shapes. Place 2 inches apart on ungreased cookie sheets. Bake 8 to 9 minutes or until set and very lightly browned. Cool 2 minutes on cookie sheets. Remove to wire racks.

3. Place 1 cup powdered sugar in shallow bowl. Roll warm cookies in powdered sugar. Cool completely. Sift remaining 1/2 cup powdered sugar over cookies just before serving.   *Makes about 4 dozen cookies*

Angel Almond Cupcakes

Grilled Banana Splits

2 large ripe firm bananas
1 teaspoon melted butter
4 tablespoons reduced-sugar, fat-free chocolate syrup
1 teaspoon orange liqueur (optional)
1 ⅓ cups sugar-free vanilla ice cream
¼ cup toasted sliced almonds

1. Prepare grill for direct cooking

2. Cut unpeeled bananas lengthwise; brush melted butter over cut sides. Grill bananas, cut-side down, over medium-hot coals 2 minutes or until lightly browned; turn. Grill 2 minutes or until tender.

3. Combine syrup and liqueur, if desired, in small bowl.

4. Cut bananas in half crosswise; carefully remove peel. Place 2 pieces banana in each bowl; top with ⅓ cup ice cream, 1 tablespoon chocolate syrup, and ¼ of nuts; serve immediately.

Makes 4 servings

St. Patrick's Mint Layered Pound Cake

1 frozen loaf pound cake (16 ounces), partially thawed
Few drops green food color (optional)
1 container (8 ounces) frozen non-dairy whipped topping (3½ cups), thawed
1 HERSHEY'S Cookies 'n' Mint Chocolate Bar (7 ounces), chopped

Slice pound cake horizontally into four layers with serrated knife. Stir green food color into whipped topping, if desired; stir in chocolate bar pieces. Place bottom cake layer on serving plate; spread about 1 cup topping mixture over layer. Repeat layers, ending with topping mixture. Cover; refrigerate. Garnish as desired. Refrigerate leftover cake. *Makes about 8 to 10 servings*

Grilled Banana Split

Black Forest Torte

**1 package DUNCAN HINES® Moist Deluxe Dark Chocolate
    Fudge Cake Mix
2½ cups whipping cream, chilled
2½ tablespoons confectioners' sugar
1 (21-ounce) can cherry pie filling**

Preheat oven to 350°F. Grease and flour two 9-inch round cake pans.

Prepare, bake and cool cake as directed on package.

Beat whipping cream in large bowl until soft peaks form. Add sugar gradually. Beat until stiff peaks form.

To assemble, place one cake layer on serving plate. Spread two-thirds cherry pie filling on cake to within ½ inch of edge. Spread 1½ cups whipped cream mixture over cherry pie filling. Top with second cake layer. Frost sides and top with remaining whipped cream mixture. Spread remaining cherry pie filling on top to within 1 inch of edge. Refrigerate until ready to serve.   *Makes 12 to 16 servings*

Tip: Chill the cherry pie filling for easy spreading on cake. Also, garnish the cake with grated semisweet chocolate or white chocolate curls.

Black Forest Torte

Decadent Layered Brownies

1 package (20 ounces) walnut brownie mix, plus ingredients to prepare mix
4 ounces cream cheese, softened
3½ cups powdered sugar
1 container (16 ounces) chocolate frosting

Preheat oven to 350°F. Lightly grease 13×9-inch baking pan.

Prepare brownie mix as directed on package for cakelike brownies. Spread in prepared pan. Bake 24 to 26 minutes or until set. Cool completely in pan on wire rack. Beat cream cheese and powdered sugar in large bowl until smooth and of spreading consistency. Spread evenly over brownies; chill. Top with frosting. Chill 2 to 4 hours. Cut into bars and serve at room temperature.　　*Makes 2 dozen brownies*

Polka Dot Macaroons

1 14-ounce bag (5 cups) shredded coconut
1 14-ounce can sweetened condensed milk
½ cup all-purpose flour
1¾ cups "M&M's"® Chocolate Mini Baking Bits

Preheat oven to 350°F. Grease cookie sheets; set aside. In large bowl combine coconut, condensed milk and flour until well blended. Stir in "M&M's"® Chocolate Mini Baking Bits. Drop by rounded tablespoonfuls about 2 inches apart onto prepared cookie sheets. Bake 8 to 10 minutes or until edges are golden. Cool completely on wire racks. Store in tightly covered container.

Makes about 5 dozen cookies

Decadent Layered Brownies

The publisher would like to thank the companies and organizations listed below for the use of their recipes and photographs in this publication.

A.1.® Steak Sauce

Bestfoods

Birds Eye®

Butterball® Turkey Company

Campbell Soup Company

Dole Food Company, Inc.

Duncan Hines® and Moist Deluxe® are registered trademarks of Aurora Foods Inc.

Eagle® Brand

Fleischmann's® Original Spread

Hershey Foods Corporation

Kikkoman International Inc.

Kraft Foods Holdings

Lipton®

©Mars, Inc. 2001

National Honey Board

Reckitt Benckiser

The J.M. Smucker Company

Southeast United Dairy Industry Association, Inc.